Disorders, Syndromes And Mental Illnesses

Harmonee Peebels

Dedication

For those with mental illness or disorders,
I see you.

Preface

This book mentions different disorders, syndromes, and
mental illnesses.
Please read at your own discretion.

Acknowledgements

I would like to thank my family for always supporting me and encouraging me to write. I would also like to thank my friends Lain, Amelia, and Tina who stuck by my side through the ups and down. I would also like to thank my teachers from high school, Ms. Gee, Mrs. Kothe, Mr. Redmond, and Mr. Webb. I also would like to offer a thank you to one of my college professors, Doctor Price. Without them I don't think I would be here and writing these poems. And finally, a special thank you to my Uncle Richard, who although may not be with us, still inspires me every day.

1. Generalized Anxiety Disorder

It hits without warning,
And not always in morning,
It can grip your heart,
And most certainly tear you apart,
It strikes unseen,
Like a killer on screen,
There are many signs,
I wish they were guidelines,
Like increased heart rate,
But it feels like a weight,
Always feeling tense,
Like when playing defense,
Feels like wrestling,
When you're trembling,
Always feeling danger,
From every stranger,
Can't help but panic,
As if I was on the Titanic,

Can't get my thoughts in order,
This is my Generalized Anxiety disorder.

2. Social Anxiety Disorder

Social interactions bring anxiety,
Anything that deals with society,
I'm too afraid to speak,
Like I'll be seen as a freak,
I want to be hidden like a needle,
Whenever there are people,
I'm scared of being rejected,
As if I'm defected,
When I talk, I'm blushing,
And it's always as if I'm rushing,
Always tripping over my words,
Or copying like mockingbirds,
I'm almost always trembling,
Did something go wrong with my assembling?
My heart is racing,
And I'm not even pacing,
I always have negative thoughts,
My insides feel tied into knots,
I can't fit into society,
Because of my Social Anxiety.

3. Restless Leg Syndrome

It can happen at any age,
And can sometimes feel like a cage,
It gets worse as you grow older,
At least it's not a lot to shoulder,
I always want to move my legs,
I can't hold them still like pegs,
It's always an urge,
I wish I could purge,
My legs are always moving,
And everyone seems disapproving,
Moving eases the discomfort,
At least it provides some comfort,
It can be passed through genetics,
It isn't just for aesthetics,
It isn't always a mystery,
If it runs in your family history,
I could take medications,
But they don't always stop the sensations,
I can sometimes tend to roam,
This is my Restless Leg Syndrome.

4. Arrhythmia

This deals with my heart,
I wish there was a restart,
My heart doesn't beat properly,
Instead, it is quite somberly,
It can feel like a fluttering,
Almost like muttering,
Or it could be pounding,
Which isn't grounding,
Or it could be racing,
And I'm not even pacing,
It could be a fast heartbeat,
Or the opposite with a slow beat,
I can have shortness of breath,
But at least it's not death,
It can be accompanied by chest pain,
Which always causes a strain,
I may have to take medications,
Which helps the sensations,
Or I may need surgery,
At least it isn't a neurosurgery,

There are so many solutions,
And many institutions,
There are many types of arrhythmias,
This is my Heart Arrhythmia.

5. Insomnia

I never seem to sleep,
I can't even count sheep,
The nights are long,
And the urge to sleep is strong,
Once asleep it can be hard to stay that way,
No matter how much I pray,
I can wake up way too early,
Or I can wake up hourly,
Sleepless nights are familiarity,
Sleeping in is a rarity,
There can be many causes,
Which all provide losses,
I can have problems staying focused,
And it mostly stays unnoticed,
It always leads to worries,
That come and go like flurries,
I always feel sleepy,
Which can make me feel needy,
There are sleeping medications,
But those may only work on some occasions,

If only there was a sense of order,
This is my Insomnia - a Sleeping Disorder

6. Sleep Paralysis

This is a different sleep disorder,
One that has no order,
It can last a few minutes,
At least it has it has its limits,
I feel awake,
But it feels fake,
I can't move,
Can't even disapprove,
I can't speak,
Not even a little squeak,
Can last months or years,
Sometimes it drives me to tears,
I see things that aren't there,
And sometimes they stare,
I can hear things,
Like the beating of wings,
I know those aren't real,
But sometimes they have an appeal,
I can sometimes see what they mean through analysis,
This is my Sleep Paralysis.

7. OCD (Obsessive Compulsive Disorder)

The urges are unwanted,
But they can often make me feel daunted,
Intrusive thoughts,
Can turn my insides into knots,
It can cause distress,
I always have to impress,
There are different categories,
And each have their own territories,
One is about cleaning,
Which always has some screening,
Another is about contamination,
Which can involve cleaning everything with no hesitation,
It could be about symmetry,
Definitely don't want asymmetry,
One is about perfection,
I may avoid looking at my reflection,
I could take medications,
But I can forget to take them on occasions,

I wish I could be out of order,
This is my Obsessive Compulsive Disorder.

8. Body Dysmorphic Disorder

It affects all genders,
Not just transgenders,
It's most common in teenage years,
And can be the cause of many tears,
The causes are unknown,
I wish they could be known,
I constantly look in a mirror,
Always finding an error,
Is that my body?
I think today I will be a homebody,
I'm constantly comparing,
I feel like everyone is staring,
I constantly avoid social events,
Feels like another episode of 'The Biggest Loser' presents,
I restrict my eating,
I don't want to be overeating,
I could take medication,
But can it really help my fixation?

Is my body really in order?
This is my Body Dysmorphic Disorder.

9. ADHD (Attention Deficient Hyperactivity Disorder)

I typically start in childhood,
Which can make me feel misunderstood,
It can cause anxiety,
Which can make me feel like an outcast in society,
I can hyperfocus,
Like it's hocus pocus,
I can be impulsive,
Which can come off as compulsive,
I can be disorganized,
But easily mesmerized,
I can be forgetful,
Which can make me fretful,
I can often have no motivations,
Yet can also have fixations,
I can often feel tired,
Yet at the same time inspired,
I often lose track of time,

Especially around bedtime,
Most treatments are medications,
Which can change even my foundations,
There is no order,
This is my Attention Deficient Hyperactivity Disorder.

10. Dyslexia

I always avoid reading,
It was something I was always dreading,
I never want to read aloud,
Even when it is allowed,
I have difficulty processing letters and their sounds,
I wish they were out-of-bounds,
I may have problems speaking,
It may come out as squeaking,
I can have problems with spelling,
It was never a subject where I was excelling,
I may have difficulty rhyming,
I can never get the timing,
Is the cause genetics?
It's definitely not for aesthetics,
What is wrong with my brain?
Why does it feel like I'm not sane?
There are no cures,
When it comes to reading, I'll always take detours,
I'll always hate word order,
This is Dyslexia, my Neurodevelopmental Disorder.

11. Bipolar Disorder

Also known as Manic-Depressive Illness,
There are never moments of stillness,
I can be very happy,
Then become snappy,
It can happen so quickly,
I can even become prickly,
I have episodes of paranoia,
And they're never pretty like the tree of sequoia,
My phases can vary,
Which can be very scary,
From sadness and crying,
Which can be horrifying,
To feeling hopeless and worthless,
Which leaves me mirthless,
I can alternate between high and low moods,
Which can affect other's attitudes,
I can take medication,
But those can be a cause of frustration,
It's like I'm always jumping different borders,
This is my Bipolar Disorder.

12. Depression

Persistent feelings of sadness,
Can often feel like madness,
Often accompanied by feelings of loss,
I can't get my feelings across,
For some, one episode may occur,
It may feel like a saboteur,
Most people will have multiple episodes,
In some cases, they can feel like codes,
I can often sleep too much,
And I don't really like touch,
I often find myself not eating,
And those moments are not fleeting,
I'd rather stay home,
Then go out and roam,
I find myself having suicidal thoughts,
They often tie my insides into knots,
I'm often given an antidepressant,
Sometimes it works as a suppressant,
To answer your question,
This is my Depression.

13. Seasonal Depression

The seasons change,
And sometimes I feel strange,
I may feel depressed when it turns fall,
Makes me want to curl into a ball,
Or it be winter,
Maybe I'm just an overthinker,
Sometimes it happens in spring,
And it isn't just a fling,
It sometimes happens in summer,
Good thing I was never a runner,
Thoughts run through my head,
They always bring some dread,
Is something wrong with me?
Maybe I should drink a cup of tea,
Is this normal?
Or am I just abnormal?
I don't want to be this way,
Please take this away,
This is, without question,
My Seasonal Depression

14. Postpartum Depression

People tell me I should be happy,
Instead of being snappy,
I just delivered a child,
I should have smiled,
I should feelings a plenty,
But instead, I feel empty,
With my child I should be bonding,
But I don't seem to be responding,
I feel rounds of sadness,
Feels like I'm spiraling into madness,
They say I'll get over it,
That the baby and I will become close-knit,
When will that happen?
I feel like I'm speaking Latin,
Do other people see I'm struggling?
Can they see me stumbling?
Does this make me a monster?
Am I another number on a roster?
Maybe one day,
It won't look so grey,

Here is my confession,
This is my Postpartum Depression.

15. Anorexia Nervosa

It affects all people,
I want to be as skinny as a crochet needle,
It doesn't care about culture or race,
And it doesn't often leave a trace,
It can happen at any age,
It's not during teenage,
It can happen with any gender,
Just to make us slender,
I restrict what I eat,
And if I eat then I cheat,
I may look thin,
Like a pin,
Or I could look overweight,
But I have lost weight,
If not treated,
I'll be defeated,
I may need medications,
Or it could lead to more complications,
It's never pretty like a mimosa,
This is my Anorexia Nervosa.

16. Bulimia Nervosa

It affects you no matter your gender,
Congratulations, you're now a contender,
Every culture and race,
No matter your status,
It could put you in hiatus,
Always have a trace,
There's no known cause,
At least it doesn't require gauze,
It's characterized by binge eating,
These moments are never fleeting,
it can be accompanied by forceful vomiting,
It seemed the most promising,
My self-esteem is negative,
Am I always sensitive?
I hate my body,
Maybe that's why I'm a homebody,
I could try therapy,
Maybe even psychotherapy,
It's never pretty like a mimosa,
This is my Bulimia Nervosa.

17. Tourette's Syndrome

It begins in childhood,
And I'm often misunderstood,
I do actions I can't control,
Which can sometimes take its toll,
My head sometimes jerks,
They can sometimes be as startling as fireworks,
I say things I don't mean,
I wish I could hide behind a screen,
I could call people names,
I really don't mean them, despite other people's claims,
It's all involuntary,
It can cause others to be wary,
Why couldn't I be normal?
Instead, I'm abnormal,
The causes aren't known,
I suppose they'll always be unknown,
I could go to therapy to help manage my tics,
But it'll never be a complete fix,
I like to spend more time at home,
This is my Tourette's Syndrome

18. PTSD (Post Traumatic Stress Disorder)

It can happen at any age,
And can often feel like a cage,
It happens after a traumatic event,
But we never know to what extent,
It could change who we are,
And there's more than just a physical scar,
It isn't about just fitness,
I could have been a witness,
I could have been involved,
There is a lot still unresolved,
It can happen from war,
Upholding the oath I swore,
It can happen from abuse,
Doesn't matter if it left a bruise,
It can happen from sexual assault,
Where we're left wondering, 'Is it my fault?'
We may withdraw,
Is that a flaw?
We'll get nightmares,

And those will always bring tears,
We'll relive those moments,
From we were up against opponents,
There is never a kind of order,
This is Post Traumatic Stress Disorder.

19. Depersonalization - derealization Disorder

In short experiences, it can be very common,
Longer experiences are uncommon,
It's feelings of being detached,
As if it never matched,
It can be detachment from myself,
Then I have no feeling of self,
This is depersonalization,
It's like an externalization,
It could be detachment from my surroundings,
It certainly wouldn't be my first founding's,
This is derealization,
And it sure can be a weird sensation,
When they happen, they can feel like a dream,
But sometimes I wish I could scream,
No one knows the cause,
I wish there was a pause,
Most choose therapy,
Which can lead to psychotherapy,

Sometimes it feels like I'm on a border,
This is my Depersonalization-derealization Disorder

20. Dissociative Identity Disorder (Multiple Personality Disorder)

Everyone has an identity,
But not everyone's is serenity,
My personality changes,
Sometimes with different exchanges,
For a little bit I'm me,
And I'll be carefree,
Then things changed,
And I can be deranged,
I don't remember this transition,
Could it be I have a condition?
Some people have multiple personalities,
Are they the abnormalities?
Each are their own person,
And sometimes they can worsen,
Sometimes there are two,
But for some, that number is few,
Sometimes there are three,

And each want to be set free,
Sometimes I'm out of order,
This is my Dissociative Identity Disorder

21. Suicide

If there's one thing these all have common,
It sure isn't a strawman,
It may not be a disorder,
But it sure does walk the border,
It may not be a syndrome,
But it never guarantees me to return home,
I can make the jokes,
But the words feel like a hoax,
It starts as thoughts,
That at first, tie my stomach into knots,
Next comes the harm,
Whether it's on the thigh or the arm,
I feel I deserve the pain,
Even when I know it's not sane,
Next, I may try pills,
And it's not for the thrills,
Sometimes I wonder,
What it'd be like to go under,
But even as my world goes dark,
My friends and family are a spark,

They keep me going,
Without even knowing,
Maybe not day I'll meet death,
But not while I still have breath.